ALSO BY SETH GODIN

Permission Marketing

Unleashing the Ideavirus

Survival Is Not Enough

the big red fez

How to Make Any Web Site Better

Seth Godin

This edition first published in Great Britain by Simon & Schuster UK Ltd, 2002
A Viacom Company

1   3   5   7   9   10   8   6   4   2

Simon & Schuster UK Ltd
Africa House
64-78 Kingsway
London WC2B 6AH

www.simonsays.co uk

Simon & Schuster Australia
Sydney

A CIP catalogue record for this book is available from the British Library

ISBN 0-7432-2086-2

Manufactured in the United States of America

For Red Maxwell

Talented, generous and a great friend

THE BIG RED FEZ

There are two versions of what happens online.

There's the engineer's version, which is that smart people, with plenty of time, who know precisely what they want from their online surfing, are able to make a considered decision with access to all the data. This version of the web says that if you can thoughtfully organize everything you can think of, people will find what they want and do business with you.

Then there's the marketer's version. This says that people are busy, ill informed, impatient, not very thoughtful and eager to click on something right now. Marketers also believe that if you don't give a prospect the right thing to click on right now, he's going to hit the "Back" button and leave.

The second version is the one that's backed up with all the data and all the successful results. Because it's the right version. The first version is what leads most web-based companies to failure.

One of the best ways to remind yourself about what's really going on is to think of a monkey in a big red fez. Now, imagine that the monkey is in some sort of bizarre psychology experiment in which the researcher is trying to train the monkey to climb a ladder and jump into a vat of lime Jell-O.

The best way to motivate the monkey, of course, is to use a banana. Whenever the monkey walks into a new situation, all it wants to know is, "Where's the banana?" If the banana isn't easy to see, easy to get and obvious, the monkey is going to lose interest. But if you can make it clear to the monkey what's in it for him, odds are he'll do what you want.

I imagine the web as a series of offer pages, all competing to get us to click. And if those sites make it really clear and obvious where the monkey's banana is, then the time-starved, not-very-bright consumer (that's you and me folks!) will go for it.

Some people might object to the characterization of web surfers as monkeys. After all, they say, we're smarter than that. No, actually, we're not. We're not smart because we're busy, or we're distracted, or we've never been to a particular site before and we're not mind readers.

Why are so many sites in financial trouble? Why is it almost impossible to get a new consumer web company funded?

The answer is deceptively simple: Because the engineers have been in charge (okay, the big-money marketers too, but that's a different book).

Face it, if you're like me, you don't really know how to build a web site and integrate it with your backend SQL database. Heck, you don't even know what a backend SQL database is. But someone in your company does know what one is (or pretends she does) and so that person has a great deal of power. In the old days of 1995, just about everyone with power on the web knew his technical stuff. These people had a software engineer's point of view. Guys like Jerry Yang or Larry Ellison are pretty hard to bluff when it comes to the technical side. The rest of us, though, are sitting ducks.

The original web designers wrote the early books, influenced the early articles, staffed the first web shops. They were the ones who founded Organic and Sapient. They loved technical stuff and viewed marketing as a necessary evil, not the center of the net.

All was fine, except when they were joined by the Hollywood-wannabes, the guys with the soul-patch beards and weird haircuts. These were the folks who wanted cool more than anything. They were encouraged by the first few million folks online, the early adopters with fast connections in search of the cool site of the day. Put the three together and you ended up with multimedia extravaganzas, or densely packed multilevel menus. In short, you got a hacker's dream.

This orgy of overprogrammed, overthought, overbuilt web sites was funded by eager-beaver venture capitalists who embraced the engineering-centric view of the web. They were used to funding technology companies, not direct-marketing companies.

So . . . cool plus efficient equals Boo.com. Cool plus nerdy equals Living.com or Furniture.com. Both are a disaster when it came to making money from the web.

Here is the old formula:

1. Raise $40 million.

2. Spend half of it on a fancy design firm working in conjunction with a fancy engineering firm (or hire the fancy people yourself).

3. Design a site that is optimized for regular users who know how your site is organized and know exactly what they want. Be sure you have a huge selection of things for them to read, do or buy.

4. Make sure your system design can support an avalanche of hits.

5. Spend the rest of the money on TV ads, portal deals and parties.

6. Raise more money.

Most people reading this book didn't follow all these steps. Perhaps you skipped steps one and five (except maybe the parties). Odds are that you still focused on getting traffic (eyeballs, hits, search engine listings) and designed a user-driven site that allowed a smart, focused, patient person to find exactly what she wanted. And then you spent whatever resources you had left building entertainment, improving the look of the site, putting in Flash and rollovers and more.

And now, alas, it's not working as well as you hoped.

Amazon.com, my favorite site in the whole world (as you'll see in the pages that follow), set a trap for the rest of us. I have no idea if they did this intentionally, but Jeff Bezos is smart enough to have pulled that off as well. What's the trap?

Amazon set an example. An example of the online catalog, the online brand, the profitable portal deal, the profitable affiliate program. I've got news for you: Just because it worked for Amazon, doesn't mean it's going to work for you.

The fact that it worked for Amazon, indeed, makes it less likely that it's going to work for you. You don't have the money. You don't have the time. Most important, Amazon has picked all the low-hanging cherries on that tree. So if you're going to make your web site work, you're going to have to work for it.

Of all the net books I've written, this is far and away the simplest. You might find it trivial. But I've never seen a site that couldn't benefit from the few insights contained herein. Enjoy it. (If you need the inspiration, you can get your very own monkey in a fez by visiting www.bigredfez.com.)

the
big
red
fez

THE BIG RED FEZ

THE PACHINKO MACHINE THEORY OF WEB BUSINESS

In Japan, there are thousands of pachinko parlors. For some reason, the obsession never caught on here, and that's a shame. It turns out that pachinko is a terrific way to think about the challenges facing web marketers.

A pachinko machine is a bit like a pinball machine, but the differences are important. First, it's upright, so the balls fall much faster. Second, you buy balls by the hundreds, and shoot them as fast as you can, with repeated twangs of your thumb on the launcher. It's called "pachinko" because of all the noise the balls make as they fall through the machine.

With all those balls in play, it doesn't really matter if a few drain out the holes in the bottom. Nobody whacks a machine or tilts it as they do with American pinball. And most balls do drain, with a few hitting the jackpot and giving free balls.

Your site is a pachinko machine. If you buy enough "balls," you'll have plenty of traffic coming in at the top of the machine. The challenge (which is totally under your control) is how to design the layout of the "machine" so that the balls—or most of them—go where you want them.

Most sites are poorly designed. They waste a lot (or sometimes, virtually all) of the balls that flow through. As a result, the owners of these sites need to pay more money for more traffic in order to get the desired results.

In this book I outline a very different theory. In essence,

it's a direct marketer's way of looking at traffic. If you can get some of the balls to go where you want, it's okay if the rest drain away.

As the balls work their way down through the machine that you call your site, you can choose to place more and more pages between them and the desired goal. Of course, the more pages you place, the more likely it is that the ball won't do what you want and will drain, leaving you with nothing.

So the challenge is to create a series of enticing offers, impenetrable boundaries and thoughtful and logical steps that keep people with you from the moment they arrive until they successfully reach the destination you've set out for them.

What's so cool about this analysis is that you soon realize that balls toward the bottom of the machine (near your goal) are worth far, far more to you than fresh balls just in on the top. You quickly find that it's okay to waste a lot of balls at the topmost level, but only if that sorting action on your part leads to more and more profit for you at the bottom.

The goal is to have a site where X percent of the balls you put in the top end up doing what you want. If you can figure out what X needs to be to make you a profit, AND you can determine how to accomplish that goal, you've built a perpetual motion machine of money.

If this sounds like direct marketing, that's because it is direct marketing. The web is a giant direct-marketing machine, and the best tactic is to use direct-marketing thinking to create a site where your margin per relationship is greater than the cost of that relationship. Where your pachinko balls make a profit!

Now that you've got a site where balls generate more revenue than they cost to buy, buy more balls. It's not rocket science. It's simple. So simple that all those sites that lost $5 or $10 or $300 on each and every person they brought in ignored it. They weren't playing pachinko. They were gambling and they lost.

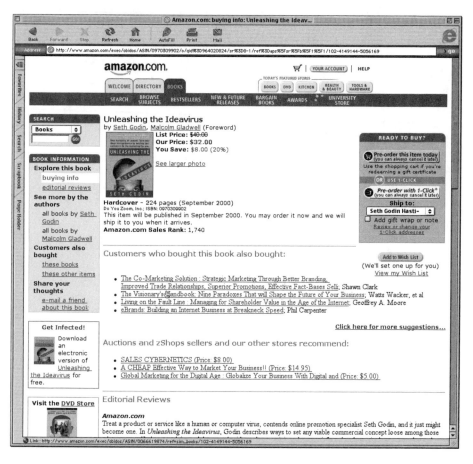

Is there any doubt where you're supposed to click? Amazon has trained all of us to know that the search is over to the left and the click to buy is on the right. In case you forget, they put a big blue box around the spot where they want you to click.

FIRST RULE OF THE BANANA

Here's what we know:

People don't visit many web pages considering how many there are.

When they do visit a page, they decide if they're going to stay in less in three seconds. If they don't know what to do, they hit the "Back" button.

The vast majority of people who visit your web site aren't going to figure out what to do in three seconds.

If you show them in a totally obvious obvious obvious way, maybe they'll figure it out. (All four paragraphs above are literally true. I didn't make them up . . . they're tested facts.)

Hence the banana (remember the fez!). Force yourself to design each and every page with one and only one primary objective. That's the banana. Make it big. Make it blue (or red). Make it obvious.

Fight the urge to be all things. Pick one thing. No, your pick won't make everyone happy. So what?

If you don't pick, they won't either.

BACK!

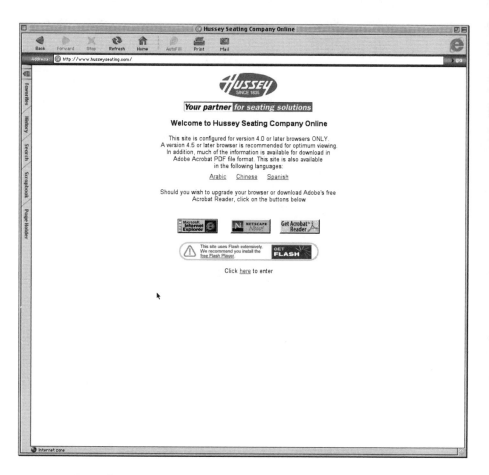

Welcome to Hussey Seating Company Online

This site is configured for version 4.0 or later browsers ONLY.
A version 4.5 or later browser is recommended for optimum viewing.
In addition, much of the information is available for download in
Adobe Acrobat PDF file format. This site is also available
in the following languages:

Arabic   Chinese   Spanish

Should you wish to upgrade your browser or download Adobe's free
Acrobat Reader, click on the buttons below

Click here to enter

*Boy, these guys are pretty confident that I really want to visit
their site. My guess is that this site is run by the IT department,
not the guys in marketing. Flash for a seating site?*

NOBODY CARES ABOUT YOU
(AS MUCH AS YOU DO)

Certainly the biggest mistake businesses make is believing that once someone has finally shown up on their site, he's going to hang out for a while and have a "virtual XYZ Corp. experience."

How often do customers show up just to shmooze with your sales force?

The page people see when they first arrive at your site (I call it a landing page) is critical to your success. Imagine what would happen to the Gap if they had a buzzer on the front door of the store in the mall! Imagine having to wait to see if you had all the proper tools—wallet? belt? underwear?—before you were let into the store!

If I have to stop, even for a click, to read some useless information, I'm going to flee. And so are your customers.

In this example, I have to look at a page that has essentially no relevance to the reason I came to the site. Hussey took an engineering-centric approach to its site. By trying to please everyone at the same time, they have virtually guaranteed that they won't have a monologue, never mind a dialogue, with most of the people who stop by looking for information.

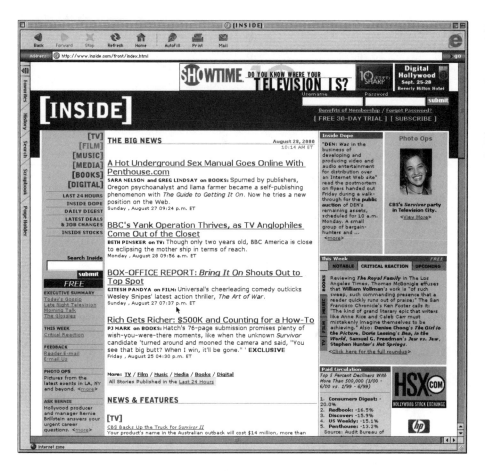

Inside.com is a great source of news and insight, but content with ads isn't enough to build a business on. Inside is short on subscribers . . . and no wonder. What are they hoping I'm going to do here? Remember, they get one banana per page.

THE BEST WAY TO GET WHAT YOU WANT

. . . is to make the banana the most obvious thing on the page. That means you have to decide what the banana is, don't you?

Most web pages have multiple goals. For example, this page wants me to:

- Search for what I'm looking for
- Find the section of the site I'm interested in
- Read one of the headlined stories
- Click on one of the advertiser's banners
- Log in
- Click on the photo of a pretty partygoer
- Subscribe

By giving me so many options, they think they've made it likely that I'll find something I like at this landing page. Of course, that assumes that I care enough to get up to speed. They've also made it likely that a stranger won't subscribe, that a regular reader won't click on a banner and that someone referred by a friend won't have a clue what to do next.

There's an alternative.

Make a different web page for every important banana. If you can segment your audience by what you know about them, you can give each group a different view of your world.

Send your nonsubscribers to a page that focuses on subscribing.

Send your first-time visitors to a more welcoming page.

Send your subscribers to a more advanced page.

This is technically straightforward and insanely profitable.

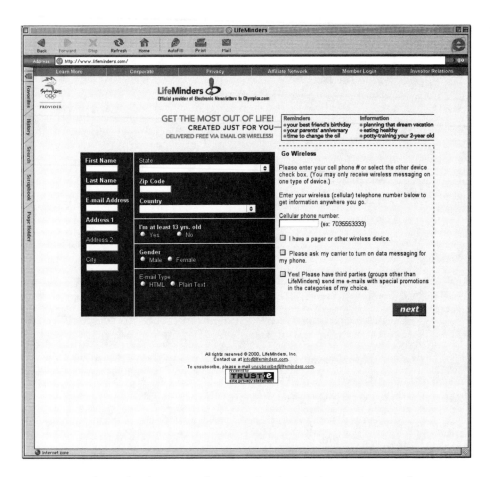

LifeMinders has a neat business idea, but they're creating one of the most common user-stumbling blocks around. Easy to fix, and it'll increase their yield.

DON'T MAKE IT EASY FOR YOU,
MAKE IT EASY FOR ME

Have you noticed that when you're busy filling out the name and address section on most sites (this being the ultimate win for the site . . . either you're ordering something or giving permission for something, which is why they built the site in the first place), they make you stop what you're doing, take your hands off the keyboard and grab the mouse?

You type your name. Your street address. Your city. Then, suddenly, there's a pull-down menu asking you to choose your state. And finally, another menu for the country. You have to scroll through Afghanistan, Lichtenstein, Oman— but don't get to Zanzibar, that's too far—and then you see United States. Hey, even if United States is at the top of the list, it's still a few extra seconds for no reason at all.

Why not just ask the person to type NY and US?

Because the engineers love using pull-down menus!

Take them out. Make it easy for the user and a little harder for the database.

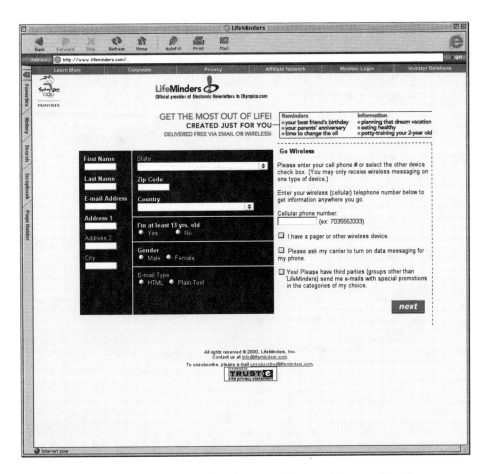

While I think it's great that these guys belong to Truste, what if I had never heard of Truste? Instead of hoping that I'll trust you, why not earn that trust by starting slow?

ONE STEP AT A TIME

Sorry to pick on these guys, but it's a good page to work with.

LifeMinders is in the business of getting subscribers to sign up for its email newsletter, then selling ads in the newsletter to people who want to read them. Great idea.

Getting subscribers is what the whole game is about, so doing this page right is the secret to their entire business. This is the money page.

So why are they asking so much? Why do they need to know my gender and my email type so soon? Can you imagine going out on a first date and saying, "Okay, before we order, I have a few questions . . . tell me your religion, how late you work most days and how many kids you hope to have . . ." Obviously a nonstarter.

Instead of asking me all this stuff right now (do I really want to give you my cell phone number—I hardly know you!) why not get the minimum? Ask for my email address. Period.

Now, you can use the next page to ask a bunch of questions, or you can send me an email with your first issue and then let me know how easy it is to give you more information so that future newsletters are even more interesting and relevant.

This step-by-step approach works. But don't take my word for it. Test it.

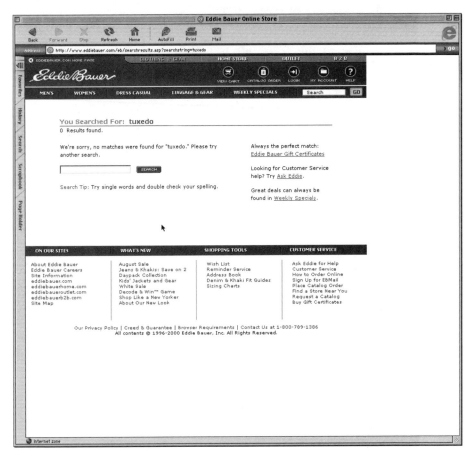

Fine. Eddie Bauer doesn't sell tuxedos. No surprise, really. But is this what happens at their store?

HI! CAN I HELP YOU?

The search engine on your site gives users a chance to tell you what they want. You worked hard to get them there. They find your site. They find the search engine. They painstakingly type in what they want.

And most of the time, they can't find a match. The search fails. So if your site is like most sites, you say, "Sorry, no matches were found." (As many as half of all online searches end in failure, mainly because people are very bad at thinking like computers.)

Is that what happens at a great retail store? You ask for collar stays and the salesperson responds, "Don't have any, sorry," and walks away.

Not likely.

Much more likely is that the salesperson says, "Collar stays! You must have a lot of trouble finding those. Do you have a minute? We're having a huge sale on 100 percent cotton shirts that don't need collar stays."

Or maybe, "Sheesh . . . we just sold our last set. Tell you what . . . find something you like in the store right now and I'll give you 10 percent off."

In the online world, why not have a failed search lead to a page that lists the ten most searched for items? Or a page of discounts? Or . . .

It doesn't always work, but why not give it a try? It's free. Remember, by the time you've got someone on this page, he is the single most valuable person you're going to see all day. He's got interest, money, and he's on your site!

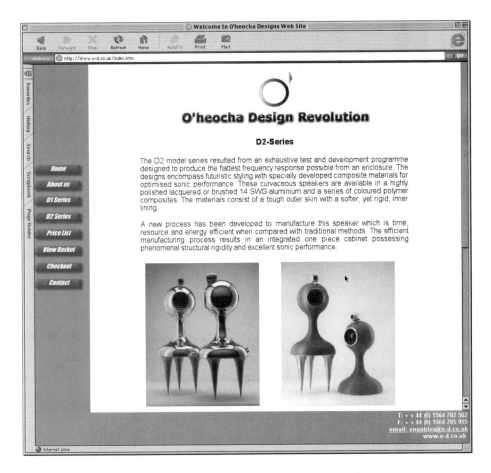

Here's the first page of a series of two. Pretty cool speakers, right? But where's the banana?!

BUY NOW!

Please don't beat around the bush with me. If I see something on your site that I want to buy, don't make me beg for it.

Think about your favorite car salesman (okay, maybe your favorite shoe salesman). You find something you like. With almost any body movement or any phrase in any language, you can indicate that you'd like to buy the item.

Where on this site am I supposed to click to actually buy one of these supercool speakers?

I figured it was "View Basket." Turn the page to find out what happened.

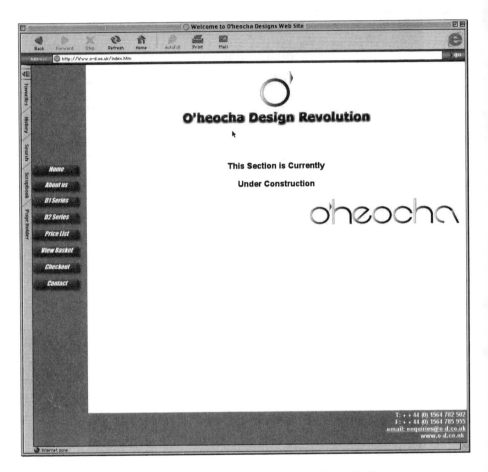

Ouch! I think it would be easier if they just took a wheelbarrow full of money, wheeled it into the street and lit it with a match.

THE BIG RED FEZ

DON'T FORGET THE SAFETY NET

Sites change. Glitches happen.

But you should never, ever have a page like this one. Don't even build it! Here I am, ready to buy speakers that cost a thousand dollars. Even though this page has been under construction for more than two months, I'm sure there's a good reason for the error message.

What's inexcusable is that an error page like this could show up without an easy, obvious way for me to raise my hand and say, "Help!"

Why don't they add the equivalent of "Press 0 to get an operator."

"Sorry, but this page isn't ready! Click here to send us an email."

A couple of years ago, when Geocities was an independent company, senior management told me that the most visited page on the entire site (at the time, the tenth most visited site on the entire web) was their error page.

More people saw the Geocities error page than any other! And of course, banners on that page had a lot of clicks (after all, they had a lot of page views). But the surprising thing is that they also did better on a percentage basis. Why? Because if you're on an error page, you're going to be much more likely to click on a banana if you think it's going to get you any closer to where you want to go.

Heat and Brew

WMF 1 1/2-Quart Stainless Steel Ball Shaped Tea Kettle with Infuser
by WMF
Our Price: $99.99

Sleekly contemporary, this mirror-finished stainless steel tea kettle honors tradition with the inclusion of a removable whistle that fits over the spout and adds a merry note to tea brewing. Otherwise, the 1-1/2-quart kettle is all business. It... Read more

Amazon.com Delivers

Sign up for Amazon.com Delivers and receive e-mail with recommendations from our editors in the following categories:

☑ Cookbooks
☑ Entertaining
☑ Kitchen News

sethgodin@yahoo.com [**Sign up**]
View all categories.

What's so clever about this permission-based sign-up? It's just one click.

DON'T ASK TWICE

Amazon knows my email address. I told them once. They didn't forget. And then they set my cookie so that they could remember me when I came back. I don't view it as an invasion of privacy. I like it!

Most sites use this sort of memory a little. Amazon manages to use it a lot. In this example, they're trying to increase the permission they have with me by getting me to sign up for weekly emails about entertaining and kitchen news ("An exciting new vegetable peeler from Oxo!").

Anyway, they prechecked the boxes for me. Nothing wrong with that, because it's not opt-out. After all, the only reason I would hit the "Sign Up" button is to sign up for a newsletter, so the precheck is a great convenience.

But far better than that is the fact that they already typed in my email address for me. Now, with one click I can subscribe. This is a good project for your engineers, who will now be less busy since you're not building Flash stuff anymore.

The only change I'd make here is their decision to use Amazon blue for the words "Sign Up," since everywhere else on the page, blue means "Click Here."

But I won't quibble. Besides, they can test to see which works better, blue or black, and use that one.

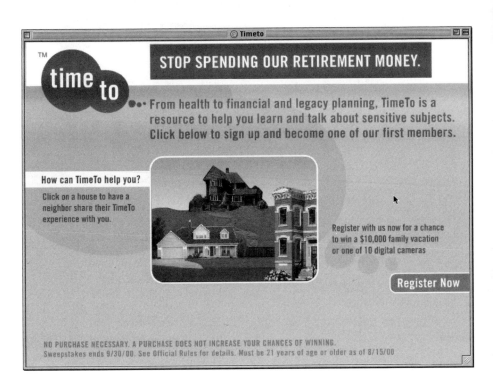

Name a successful site on the web that uses metaphors.

DIGITAL METAPHOR IS THE ENEMY OF PROGRESS

What if your car were built with little horse-and-buggy metaphors sprinkled throughout the dashboard and pedals? The steering wheel could have little reins on it. The gas pedal could go under your heel and you could jangle it, like spurs, whenever you wanted to move faster. You can imagine what the exhaust pipe would look like . . .

Every time computer designers use metaphors, they inhibit our understanding of how this new thing actually works. For example, on this site, you click on the house to hear what your neighbors are saying. Get it? Neighbors live in houses, you click on their door and they talk.

This site has a few growing pains. In addition to the troubled metaphor, they never really make it clear why you're here or what you're going to get out of it, and then, just to make things more confusing, they add a promotion (win a vacation) that's poorly described and not very relevant.

I'm certain that great content and useful solutions are deep within this site. But this landing page isn't helping me find them.

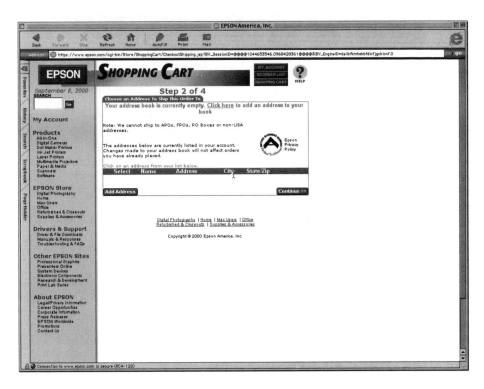

I'm sure the engineers thought they were being consistent, but can you imagine this happening in the real world?

LET THEM LOOK ALL THEY WANT

I needed some transparencies for my new Epson 1270 printer, which I love. Since Outpost and Staples didn't have them, I decided to buy them direct from Epson.

In order to even find out how much they cost, I had to register with Epson. Why on earth would I have to do that?

The engineers worked very hard to have an orderly site, with clearly labeled steps. It all works great in theory, but a real person is going to be annoyed to discover that he can't start shopping without having an account. Does Epson really need registered users?

If you're running paymybills.com, a site people visit frequently, that's one thing. But it's hard to imagine the vast majority of Epson customers wanting that sort of intimate relationship with Epson.

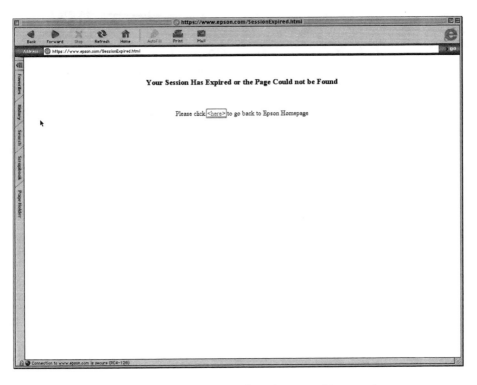

So I've got my wallet out, I'm ready to buy something . . . boom.

THE BIG RED FEZ

YOU CAN'T TEST EVERYTHING

But you can certainly test the money path. I worked my way through most of the transaction and then I got this note.

See my earlier comments about error pages. They could have done a lot to make me feel better ("Here's a five dollar coupon. Sorry we screwed up!") and make sure that I actually ended up buying something.

But most important: Test the most important paths on your site. Do it every day, just to be sure it's still working. One site I built was doing great, and then one day, someone noticed that the orders weren't coming through. Turned out an engineer fixing a small problem had replaced a file. Unfortunately, the brilliant marketer (me) had mistyped the name of the new file, and so the whole thing fell apart. My mistake. Worse still: The side effect was that the single most important part of the page was broken.

Most of your visitors aren't going to take the time to tell you about your glitches. (There's another thing to put on your error pages! "Tell me you saw this page please . . .") So it's up to you to go through the cycle at least once a day. Just in case.

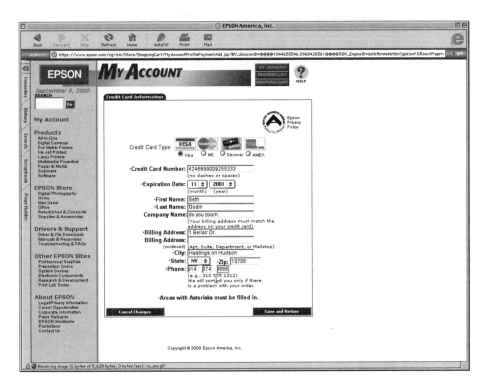

Don't ask me to do work the computer could just as easily do. If you know my zip code, just look up the town and ask me to confirm it.

IF THE COMPUTER IS SO SMART, WHY AM I DOING ALL THE WORK?

By some estimates, half of all online shopping carts are abandoned before the purchase is made. Some studies say 60 percent. Why is this? Marketers are racking their brains. I mean, try to imagine a grocery store in which 60 percent of the carts are abandoned just before the checkout. All that melting ice cream!

One big reason is that checking out from an online merchant is a major pain in the neck. Sites clutter up the process, and by the time buyer's remorse sets in, I'm still checking out. So I leave.

Here, Epson is asking me for my billing address. I already told them my shipping address. So why why why isn't there a button that says, "Billing and shipping are the same."

The computer already knows my shipping address. So why is it asking me twice?

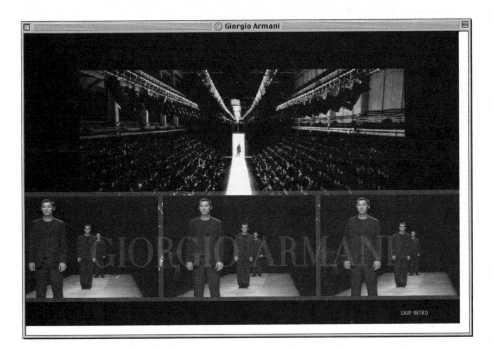

You knew this one was coming, but I couldn't help myself. Here is Giorgio Armani indulging in a high-bandwidth Flash showcase. Why?

THE BIG RED FEZ

HEY, IT REALLY ISN'T TV! REALLY.
IT'S NOT. STOP IT ALREADY.

Some people still don't get it. It costs a lot of money to make a nifty site. It costs a ton of money to make a flashy one.

Here's a TV-like commercial from Giorgio Armani. I'm sure you can see an updated version at www.giorgioarmani.com (don't spell Giorgio wrong or you won't find this site . . . but that's a different riff).

So, let me understand. Someone (probably at work) is going to point his high-bandwidth connection and fast processor (with all plug-ins installed) at this site to watch this ad for haute couture. Why?

If they did the math, Armani would understand that the cost of being constantly hip and current with this site is enormous. If they tested and tracked, they'd discover that it's doing them almost no good at all.

Rule of thumb: If it wouldn't work well as a direct-response mail piece, it's hard to understand why it's going to work well online.

So what should they do instead?

Why not build a simple site that lets loyal customers sign up, by email and zip code, for announcements? Armani might then announce a made-to-measure sale. Or send a note inviting people to look at stills of the latest collection. Or best of all, they could realize that they have a lot of fans in Cincinnati and use that data to bring a fashion show to Burdine's. That's an asset worth some money.

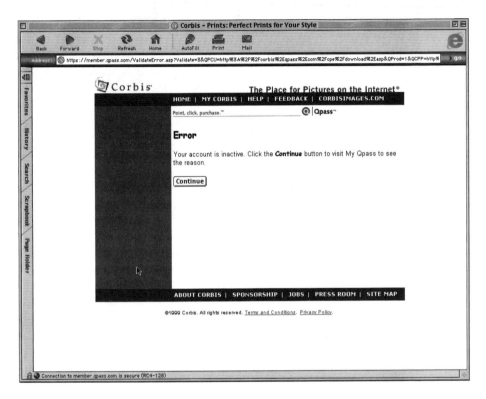

Hey! If you know why my account is inactive, TELL ME! And let me fix it with one step, not three. Thank you.

CAREFUL WHAT YOU OUTSOURCE

If you run a site that sells stuff, it's tempting to sign up with one of those universal wallets. They take care of all the hassles of charging people money and you can concentrate on making something people want to buy.

Now, I dearly love Corbis.com. I'm a big customer: I recommend them and use their stuff all the time.

I got this message during a time when Corbis outsourced the critical billing step to Qpass. And Qpass faces a catch-22. Most sites won't use them until they get really big, and they can't get really big until most sites use them. As a result, they're struggling to create a bulletproof solution.

So there I was at Corbis. I'd selected a photo from one of the millions they license. I had an account. I clicked "Buy." And I got this error message.

Ouch.

Can you think of ten ways to make this page better?

Wait a minute! Just one minute! You just told me that you were going to tell me what was wrong with my account. Now, on the very next page, you break your promise.

THE BIG RED FEZ

KEEP YOUR PROMISES

Building tension from page to page is very smart. Telling people, "Click here to find out XYZ" is a great way to get people to click on that banana.

But don't promise me something and then leave me hanging!

As you can see, clicking on the page that promised me the reason my account is inactive brought me to a standard sign-in page.

At the very least, this page should KNOW what you just promised me, and if it can't keep the promise, it should tell me why. "In order to update your account, we need you to sign in again. Sorry for the inconvenience."

You see, quite frankly, I couldn't care less why your system isn't able to tell me what I need to know. I'll just leave and go to ditto.com. And I probably won't even bother telling you why I left.

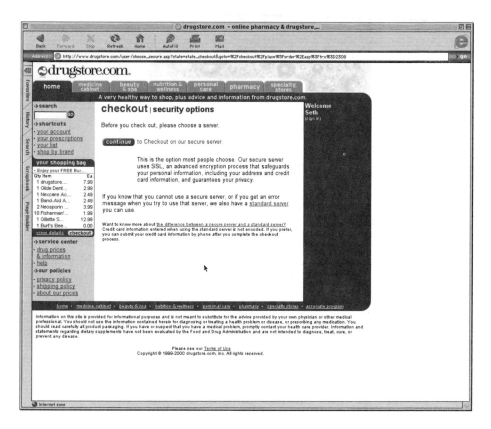

Do you walk to school or take your lunch? Cryptic questions aren't easily answered. I don't want any security options. I want the best security! And if I have to have security options, shouldn't I have a choice of more than one?

THE DREADED CHECKOUT, REVISITED

Remember that statistic about abandoned carts? Here's another great example. Drugstore.com just went through enormous hoops to get me to this page. They ran a promotion through the mail. They gave Amazon.com a boatload of stock. They organized and ran an excellent site.

And now, here I am, ready to go.

Then they ask me to do something that makes me feel stupid. "Choose your server."

This makes me feel stupid for a few reasons:

1. They only give me one choice.

2. I don't know the difference between different types of servers.

3. If I've got time to read the fine print, I suddenly get paranoid, because the fine print reminds me that bad guys are about to steal my credit card and my identity and God-knows-what else.

Instead: Assume I want the best kind of server. If that doesn't work, make it easy for me to switch to the kind that will.

What a great site! What cool stuff! What do I do now?

MORE BANANA RIFFS

This is a very handsome page. I love the endorsements that come from the client list on the bottom. I like the four pictures, the page loads quickly and shows me the gestalt of the site.

But what do I do now?

Is it all equally important? If I walked into their store, would they talk for five minutes before asking me what I'm interested in?

Are "Products" and "Search" just as important as "Get Catalog" and "About DWR"? The most common place to click on any web page is the top left-hand corner (you can look it up), yet these guys are using the top left-hand corner for nothing. Not only that, they put the most arresting graphic on the whole page there.

I think testing would show that the two most common reasons to visit their home page are either to do a search right now or to see some of their top-selling items (with pricing). Why not alternate with these two as lead banana and see which works?

What a great site! Nuff said.

PERMISSION PLUS SPEED PLUS BANANA . . .

Thought you might like to see something elegant. Here's a page from Eazel.com (cool logo, but how do I type a schwa into my browser?). Eazel was a casualty of the dot-com meltdown, but that doesn't change the quality of this site.

It loads in seconds. It answers my main question in one easy-to-find and -read paragraph. It's designed to make it clear that they're a professional organization.

And there's a banana! It says they're doing something cool. Do I want to hear more about it? So I type my email address and—boom—they've built an asset. Now, if I want to explore a bit, I can.

I don't understand why every single corporation (non-etailer) on the web isn't doing something just like this. Easy to build, easy to maintain, easy to test, creates a profit as you go.

Go figure.

Back Forward Stop Refresh Home AutoFill Print Mail

http://www.naturesflavors.com/cgi-bin/shopcart.cgi

Final total: $41.13

Please fill in all fields to insure prompt processing of your order.
Fields in bold type are required.

About You

seth godin

sethgodin@yahoo.com

914 674 9668

Name

Email address

Phone (in case there's a problem)

Organization or company

The order you are placing qualifies for our special offer. Please choose your free item below.

Peppermint Essential Oil 1 oz.

Shipping Information - WE CANNOT SHIP TO POST OFFICE BOXES

1 Bellair Dr.

Hastings on H

NY

1070

Street Address

Apartment or Suite number

City

State

5 digit zip code

Payment Information
● Credit Card [Number taken on step 4(secure)]
○ Check [Our address is on step 3]

If you've been given a special code, enter it in the box below. (Any discounts are taken after the order process)

Any comments?

How did you find out about us? Select One

Next Reset

Nature's Flavors.com

Internet zone

Did you ever get a really good clerk at Bloomingdale's or the Gap? This is her, in digital form.

BOY, THIS IS A GOOD CHECKOUT

This is me-mail! This is a page that is all about me, answers MY questions, asks for nothing more than it needs.

It gives me a free gift, which is a nice incentive to buy right now, because if I abandon my cart, I might not get that free gift.

It talks to me without talking down to me.

It makes it easy for me to share my comments. (I hope someone reads them. I bet they do.)

No pull-down menus for state, and they didn't even bother to ask my country. Good for them.

Yes, I got the tea I ordered. What a pleasure. Copy them.

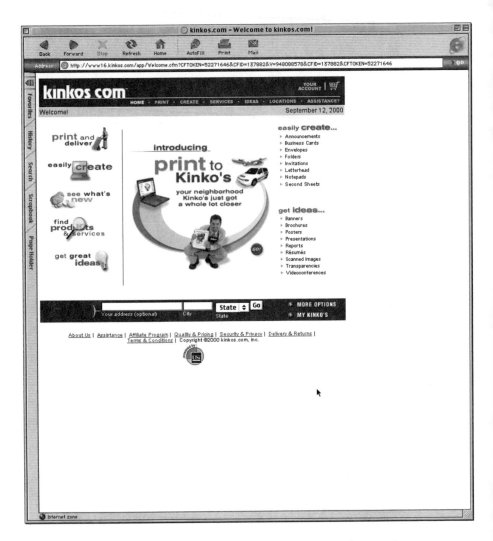

Don't forget: Screwdrivers outsell Swiss Army knives. Just because it's versatile doesn't mean it's the best way to get the job done. Think about WHY I'm here before you give me choices.

HOW MUCH IS THAT DOGGY . . .

Kinko's was doing some pretty amazing things with Kinkos.com. Create a file, click a few buttons, they print it out and deliver it to you.

Cool.

So I'm working on this book and decide I need forty color copies. That's about two thousand pages. A decent order, you would think. I wonder how much that would be? Is it worth sending it out or should I just run my Epson all night?

Click on over to Kinko's. Click on the obvious buttons. Get to this page.

Now what do I do? The banana . . . where is it?

I don't want to create. I've already created. I don't need ideas. Lord knows I've got too many of those. I know! "Print and deliver."

But when I click on this, I follow a path that leads me to a way to upload my file . . . How much is this going to cost?

Nowhere, as far as I can tell, do they ever price my job, nor do they ever tell me that they won't price my job until I submit it.

It's hard for me to imagine a real-world store with a similarly arcane way of communicating. This site is a marvel. They just forgot to make it about me.

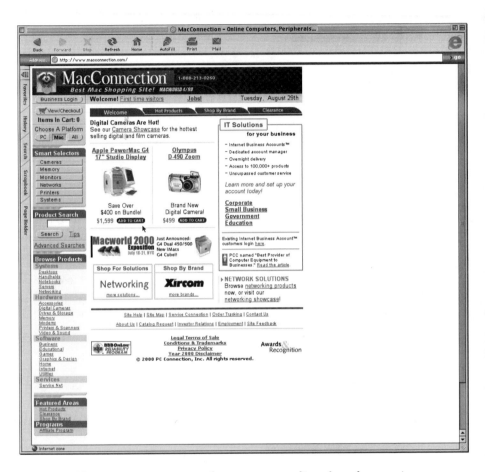

You can move your catalog customers online, but that won't increase your customer base, and it may even cost you customers. Why? Because once someone is online, she's only a click away from your competition.

THE WEB IS NOT A CATALOG

I placed my first order with MacConnection in 1985, soon after they opened. I love them. It makes me cry when I think about how much I've spent on (now) obsolete Macs and accessories over the years.

So I want to do business with them, and I want to do it online if it's fast and easy. But the web isn't the same as a mail-order catalog.

When I come to their site, I want to type in what I want and get a beautifully thought-through list of alternatives, sorted by what's best for me. I'm not going to browse through the site the way I do with their catalog—I can't fit their site in my briefcase and it's hard to get a laptop into the bathtub.

So organize your site the way a real person is going to use it, not the way you'd like the metaphor to work. Make the "Search" button the biggest banana. If you must encourage me to browse, show me bestseller lists or other information-based data that saves me time.

Simplify, simplify. It's all here. Get rid of the other stuff.

Nice work on the incentive. But why are my phone number and title "required"?

TAKE A BREATH

Remember how freaked out people got about the census? If you got the long form, the first thing you noticed was that it went on for pages and pages. I got angry. The thought of working my way through all that data was just too daunting. Only my fear of spending time in Sing Sing led me to actually fill it out.

This page, while pretty clean, makes a similar mistake. By showing me all the questions at once ("How did you hear about us?" Why should I bother telling you that!), I'm daunted. The excellent discount offer at the top keeps me going—I figure if I were ever going to buy this thing, it should be now—but they could have made it more fun.

How?

By dividing this into a few screens. Give me encouragement as I go. Automatically fill in blanks with good guesses. Give me a reward for answering nonessential questions.

How many pages? I have no idea. Test it.

NaturesFlavors.com™
Get back to Nature™

Thank you for your order! We are confident that you will enjoy the products you have just ordered.

We value each and every one of our customers, and we will do whatever it takes to make sure your visit with us is a pleasant one.

If there is anything we can do to help you, or you have any questions about your order, please do not hesitate to send us an email.

Direct questions and comments to comments@naturesflavors.com

Direct technical questions to webmaster@naturesflavors.com

We hope to see you again soon!

Back to Nature's Flavors Home

Nature's Flavors, Inc.
1145 Shelly Court
Orange, CA 92868

Nature's Flavors.com™

Nature's Flavors.com gladly accepts Visa, MasterCard, American Express, Discover, checks, and money orders
100% Secure...Guaranteed
Information presented on this web site is for educational purposes only;
statements about products and health conditions have not been
evaluated by the U.S. Food & Drug Administration.
Copyright and Disclaimer © 1999 Nature's Flavors.com §

Close, so close. But not quite a cigar.

PLEASE SAY "THANK YOU"

Okay, so you're done. You've got my money. Now what?

Most sites just give up. "Thank you." Two words or a few more on a white screen. What a waste.

Dev Bhatia at HotSocket.com has discovered that the thank-you page is one of the most valuable on the entire site. I just bought from you. You haven't screwed up. I'm glowing. Quick, before buyer's remorse sets in . . . sell me something else.

"Thanks! We appreciate your business. Click here to save ten dollars, right now, on any lipstick we carry."

Or:

"Thanks! We appreciate your business. We thought you might like to be introduced to Fred's Fly Factory. If you click here, you can save 10 percent on anything in his store." I mean, hey, you've already collected my credit card data. I'm raring to spend money!

You get the idea.

This is a wonderful page from a nice company. I love the way they make it easy for me to contact them to follow up. But they can (and should) take the relationship much farther. This is the moment.

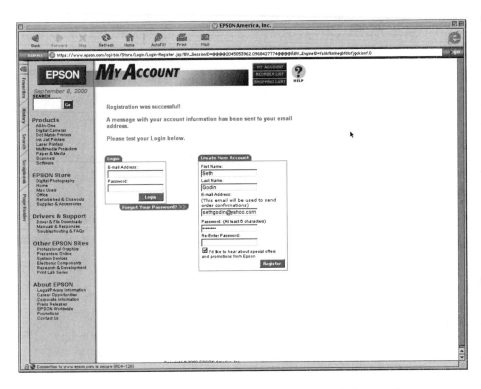

Try very hard not to ask someone to leave your site before you let him do business with you.

THE BIG RED FEZ

DON'T BUY NOW ...

I'm picking on Epson because it's easy (I got all the screen shots in one visit), but also because these are very common mistakes.

Here we see that Epson is requiring registration to shop.

And in order to register, you've got to actually leave the site, check your email and then come back.

Some people don't get their email so fast. What if it takes ten minutes or a day for that registration information to get to me? Am I really going to wait all that time to make my first purchase with Epson? I don't even know the price!

Why do they need this level of security? Yes, someone could be forging an email address in order to do business with them, but why? Who's it helping? It sure isn't helping me.

(By the time you read this, I bet Epson has overhauled this process. Probably worth a visit.)

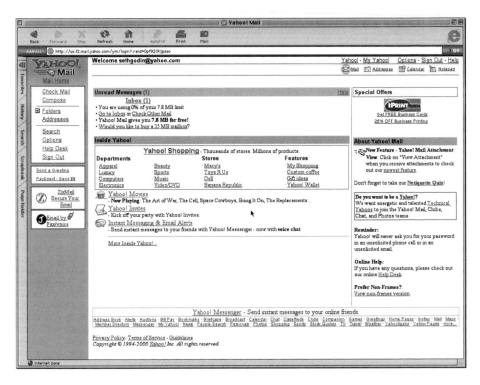

Redundancy is often the enemy of a great web experience. If you know where someone wants to go, take her there!

PLEASE GET OUT OF MY WAY

David Filo, the cofounder of Yahoo!, is absolutely brilliant about the user experience. Yahoo's pages load faster and are easier to understand than almost any other site on the web.

That's why this page, one of the most visited on the site, is so surprising.

Let's say I have a Yahoo! mail account.

Let's say I want to check my mail. I go to my home page: my.yahoo.com. The mail flag tells me I have a message. I click on the flag. It takes me to this page.

Where am I going to click?

Of course, I'll click on the "Inbox" button. That's why I came. To check my mail! Why would click on anything else? Can you imagine clicking on the button to check your mail, getting to this page and then deciding to click on, say, "Dell." I can just hear you: "I'm going to check my mail. Wait! I think I'll buy a new computer by clicking on this tiny blue link instead."

You'd better have a very good reason before you get in the path of a consumer on a mission. I can think of one thousand ways that Yahoo! could make a lot of money from this page at the same time they make consumers happy—mostly by offering truly beneficial discounts and special offers worth a distraction. Yahoo! is doing that with their shopping links as fast as they can. But not here, not yet.

If a page is just filler, and it adds a click between the consumer and what he wants, rip it out of his path.

If you forget to ask permission when someone first signs up with you, it's really, really difficult to ask for permission later. And the best way to do it is not by tricking people with a subject line like "Daily Update on your Account."

SPAM IS IN THE EYE OF THE BEHOLDER

I get asked this question more than almost any other: What's my definition of spam?

I don't have one. Instead, I define unsolicited commercial email as whatever the recipient defines as unsolicited.

Here, for example, is an email from Schwab. Yes, I use Schwab for a debit card and some basic money market accounts. No, I've never traded a stock with them, never signed up for a stock trading service and never asked them to contact me by email.

Now, I'm sure some semidesperate brand manager at Schwab, eager to make her quarter, can justify this email. After all, I do have an account with them. And she did make it easy for me to unsubscribe (the letter claims that inaction on my part leads to no subscription).

But still . . .

I trust Schwab a lot less now. I'm less likely to read their mail now. I'm less likely to sign up for something new now.

Did the brand manager get a 5 percent sign-up rate? Probably. Was it profitable, at least in the short run? Definitely. But some day, they'll realize that it cost them something big with the other 95 percent of their customer base.

```
┌─────────────────── NET RETURNS: Snap, Xoom, Gone! NBCi Relaunches ────────┐
│  ◀        ➡       ✉       ✉       ✉       🗑       ⬥ ▾                      │
│ Previous  Next   Reply  Reply All Forward  Delete Attachments               │
├─────────────────────────────────────────────────────────────────────────┤
│    From:  "TheStandard.com" <net_returns@reply.thestandard.com>             │
│    Date:  Wed, Sep 27, 2000, 8:24 PM                                        │
│      To:  sethgodin@yahoo.com                                               │
│ Subject:  NET RETURNS: Snap, Xoom, Gone! NBCi Relaunches                    │
├─────────────────────────────────────────────────────────────────────────┤
│ =============================================================               │
│                  THE INDUSTRY STANDARD'S                                    │
│                    N E T R E T U R N S                                      │
│             Your Guide to Products and Technologies                         │
│             That Create Profitable Web Businesses                           │
│ =============================================================               │
│                         | http://www.thestandard.com |                     │
│ Wednesday, September 27, 2000                                               │
│                                                                             │
│ WEEKLY FEATURES:                                                            │
│ * True Stories: NBCi Relaunches Its Web Site                                │
│ * Reboot: Track 'Em and Serve 'Em                                           │
│                                                                             │
│ ALSO THIS WEEK:                                                             │
│ * You Talkin' to Me? Virtual service reps have a lot to learn               │
│                                                                             │
│ GADGET:                                                                     │
│ * Apple's Pro Mouse                                                         │
│                                                                             │
│ /=-=-=-=-=-=-=-=-=-=-=-=-=-=-=-=-=-= advertisement =-=-=\                    │
│                                                                             │
│ Eye contact. Handshake. Done deal. Bring the confidence of one-on-one       │
│ interactions to your eMarketplace with the Question.com Collaborative       │
│ Commerce solution. Designed to create Commerce Networks of buyers and       │
│ sellers through interactive participation and decision-making, the          │
│ Question.com solution is helping companies like GE, NECX, NetworkOil        │
│ and MetalMaker. How can the new Question.com Version 3.0 transform           │
│ your eMarketplace? Visit http://www.question.com/isnr/9_27/ to find out.     │
│                                                                             │
│ \=-=-=-=-=-=-=-=-=-=-=-=-=-=-=-=-=-=-=-=-=-=-=-=-=-=-=-=/                    │
│                                                                             │
│                                                                             │
│ TRUE STORIES                                                                │
│ ~~~~~~~~~~~~                                                                │
│ Snap, Xoom, Gone! NBCi Relaunches                                           │
│                                                                             │
│ By Jenny Oh                                                                 │
│                                                                             │
│ NBCi.com just launched a new version of its Web site, integrating           │
│ brand name portals Xoom.com and Snap. Registered members of Xoom and        │
│ Snap are now redirected to NBCi.com, where the San Francisco-based          │
│ company will try to leverage original news and network content. We          │
│ spoke with Leo Chang, chief technology officer of NBCi, about the           │
│ challenges of consolidating several Internet properties into one.           │
│                                                                             │
│ The Industry Standard: What's the overall mission of the relaunched         │
│ NBCi.com?                                                                   │
│                                                                             │
│ Leo Chang: We've brought together disparate brands like Xoom and Snap       │
│ into one Web site. For instance, there used to be a search engine and       │
└─────────────────────────────────────────────────────────────────────────┘
```

Home run. An anticipated, personal and relevant weekly missile.
I read it. The ads work. They make money. Everyone is happy.

IT'S ALL ABOUT ME, REALLY, ISN'T IT?

Here's a reader-centric email newsletter that takes a little of my permission (I subscribed to the *Industry Standard,* a print magazine) and gradually leverages it into more and more permission.

First they offered me a free subscription to this newsletter. Cool.

Then they filled the newsletter with worthwhile articles that I'm delighted to read. Even better.

Now they sell ads to interesting companies with relevant offers that I may just click on. And you can bet that if I do, I'm a qualified visitor, not someone who was tricked into clicking.

Finally, they are gradually working their way up to getting me to attend a conference or two. And of course, the profit on attendance at a conference is about two hundred times greater than the profit on reading an issue of the magazine.

Note the little things. The newsletter is very well formatted. It's easy to read. It isn't filled with funny characters or bad HTML links. It's easy to subscribe and unsubscribe. The subject line doesn't try to trick me. Instead, it tells the truth and makes it easy for me to decide if I want to read this issue.

Nice work.

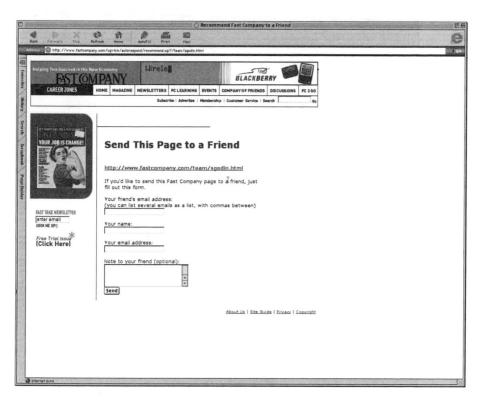

Do something cool. Make it easy to spread. And then get out of the way.

MAKE IT EASY TO SPREAD THE NEWS

This page seems so simple. You find something you like, you want to share it. Fast Company makes it easy to do. And the letter that arrives is beautifully formatted, and it's from you.

You win, because your friends think more highly of you for spreading cool ideas.

And your friends win, 'cause they get to read interesting stuff.

Of course, it's the marketer who really wins.

Previous Next Reply Reply All Forward Delete Attachments

From: "steve garfield" <sgarfield@people2people.com>
Reply-To: <sgarfield@people2people.com>
Date: Tue, Nov 7, 2000, 5:57 PM
To: "Seth Godin" <sethgodin@flashcom.net>
Subject: National Discount Brokers... business is up by 75%

I guess they got the business from the duck quack anyways:

"Millions dial freephone number - to hear duck quack

Millions of people have called a US financial company's freephone number to hear a duck quack - costing the firm $10,000 (£7,000) a day.

But bosses at the National Discount Brokers Group in Jersey City, New Jersey, don't mind footing the bill for the calls because business is up by 75%.

The company has a mallard duck as its mascot, and ended up with the quacking telephone message when president and chief executive Chris McQuilkin made it the last option on the company's automated phone system for fun.

Six million people dialled the firm's number in the last three weeks, when NDB added thousands of new accounts.

Up to 475,000 people were dialling the service each day to hear the duck quack after an e-mail message boosted the craze.

McQuilkin, whose company is being bought by Deutsche Bank, says paying for the toll-free numbers is money well spent, as the firm opened 75% more brokerage accounts in the past three weeks than it did in the previous month, CNet News.Com reports.

Last updated: 18:06 Monday 6th November 2000."

http://www.ananova.com/news/story/sm_107813.html?nav_src=newsindexHeadline

--Steve
Visit my new web site:
http://humorinthenews.weblogs.com/

Time is money. Except when we're wasting it. These guys created an ideavirus of wasted time, and then managed to convert some of that goofing off into new customers!

START A CONVERSATION

You've probably heard this story, but it's worth telling because it's such a huge success opportunity for you.

The biggest win you can create when you interact with a customer is actually not closing a sale. The biggest win is getting someone to tell ten friends, who then come do business with you.

Create conversations between your customers! I call it unleashing an ideavirus, and I wrote a book about it. But more on that later.

What National Discount Brokers did seemed dumb at first, but I was wrong and they were right.

They created a voice-mail system (call 1-800-888-3999) that sounded ordinary until you got to the last option, where you could hear a duck quack.

It was an oddball stunt, but so well executed that plenty of people told plenty of people to call them and hear the duck quack. The end result, as you can see from this email, is that their business is up 75 percent!

The added expense was from incoming phone calls where folks hung up. But the masses of traffic turned into sales and made the whole thing profitable. Wow.

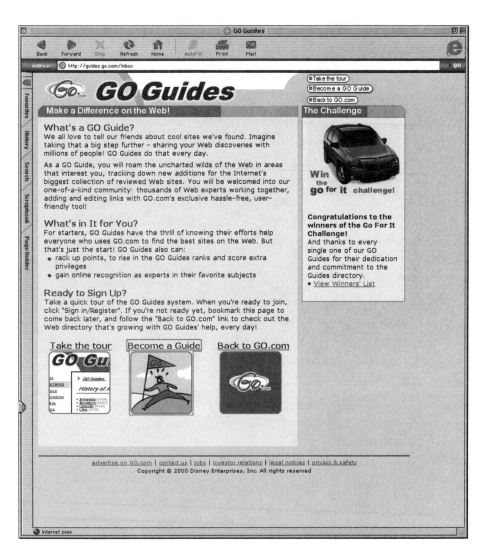

GO Guides

http://guides.go.com/Inbox

GO Guides

○ Take the tour
○ Become a GO Guide
○ Back to GO.com

Make a Difference on the Web!

The Challenge

What's a GO Guide?
We all love to tell our friends about cool sites we've found. Imagine taking that a big step further - sharing your Web discoveries with millions of people! GO Guides do that every day.

As a GO Guide, you will roam the uncharted wilds of the Web in areas that interest you, tracking down new additions for the Internet's biggest collection of reviewed Web sites. You will be welcomed into our one-of-a-kind community: thousands of Web experts working together, adding and editing links with GO.com's exclusive hassle-free, user-friendly tool!

Win the go for it challenge!

What's in It for You?
For starters, GO Guides have the thrill of knowing their efforts help everyone who uses GO.com to find the best sites on the Web. But that's just the start! GO Guides also can:

- rack up points, to rise in the GO Guides ranks and score extra privileges
- gain online recognition as experts in their favorite subjects

Congratulations to the winners of the Go For It Challenge!
And thanks to every single one of our GO Guides for their dedication and commitment to the Guides directory.
- View Winners' List

Ready to Sign Up?
Take a quick tour of the GO Guides system. When you're ready to join, click "Sign in/Register". If you're not ready yet, bookmark this page to come back later, and follow the "Back to GO.com" link to check out the Web directory that's growing with GO Guides' help, every day!

Take the tour **Become a Guide** **Back to GO.com**

advertise on GO.com | contact us | jobs | investor relations | legal notices | privacy & safety
Copyright © 2000 Disney Enterprises, Inc. All rights reserved

Internet zone

Quick, in five seconds or less: Tell me what this is about!

THE BIG RED FEZ

WHAT'S IN IT FOR ME? (YOU HAVE FIVE SECONDS)

This page no longer exists, but it's still worth talking about.

Here's a program so complicated it takes a full page just to explain enough to get you to start on a tour of the thing!

I'd have to be awfully motivated to sit through all this.

Rule of thumb: Make it easy to start, easy to keep going, easy to finish and easy to stay with. The minute it's not easy, lazy people will flee. And everyone is lazy sometimes.

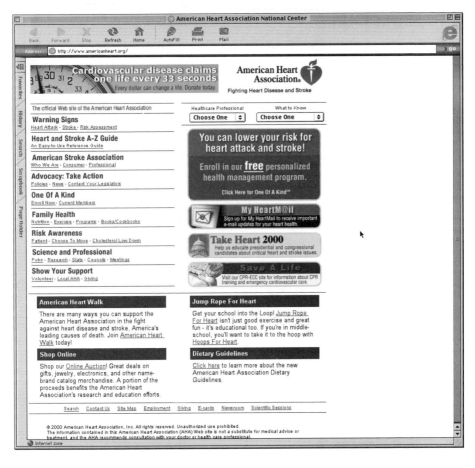

Great work from a nonprofit.

POW!

Here's a great page from the American Heart Association.

Where's the banana? Even a monkey could see it's that box in the center, right near the top *("You can lower your risk for heart attack and stroke!")*.

And best of all, the banana leads to a permission program, so they can extract long-term value out of just one visit.

I also love the way they use the word "free." Combine that with the credibility of the American Heart Association and you've got something here.

With a long complicated name like American Heart Association, though, I think they should think hard about having a second URL, something that would be easier to mention to your friends. Certainly, keep the "real" one, but register Ilovemyheart.com or something easy to remember as well. Just a thought.

A member of what?

MEMBERSHIP HAS ITS PRIVILEGES

American Express proved to us that people love to join. Somehow, they persuaded us that becoming a member of American Express was almost as much fun as joining an exclusive country club. While joining most marketing clubs is hardly membership, marketers pretend it is. Test this idea. If "membership" works, good for you.

But on this site, it gets in the way of their goal, I think. After all, these guys sell speakers that play underwater, the sort of thing you'd put in a swimming pool or a spa.

So why, exactly, do I want to be a member? Do I get a card and a secret handshake? Do we have meetings?

It seems to me that they want to either sell you on getting a free brochure or sell you the thing itself, right here, right now. I'm betting most people never ever want to hear from these guys again. Not much of a membership!

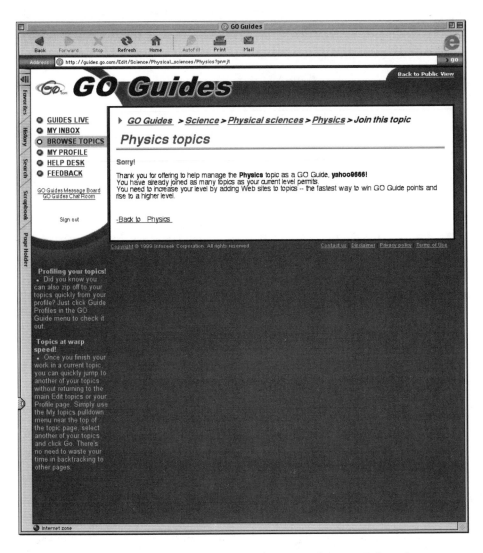

Why not have a link taking me to the areas where you DO need guides? This page is begging me to hit my "Home" button and disappear forever.

DON'T MAKE PROMISES YOU CAN'T KEEP

Back to Go.com again.

This page really annoyed me. I took all the time to read the description and qualifications of their "guide" service. I decided it might be fun to try it out, so I looked over all their choices of areas where I could be a guide.

I figured they probably had plenty of guides for really popular stuff like hopscotch or stamp collecting, so I clicked on "Physics."

This is the page I got.

Someone please tell me why they even bothered to list Physics on the previous page if they didn't have any slots available!

Surely, if the computer is smart enough to figure out that there's no room in Physics, it shouldn't list Physics.

This is why sites like this work better if they're built by hand, not by computer. A real person would have just listed the one hundred areas in which they most need people, not tried to create a complete list, only to have users find that it's useless.

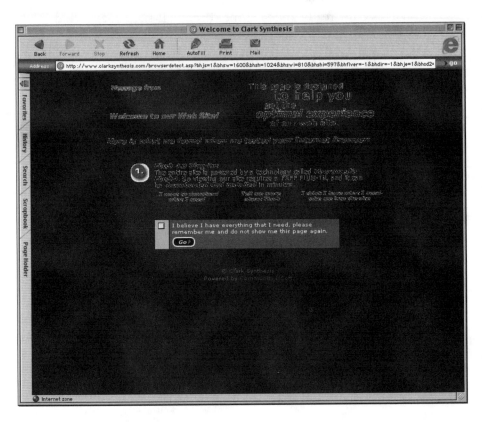

Yes, this is the actual layout of the page. It's this hard to read on top of everything else.

THE BIG RED FEZ

DON'T USE A HAMMER WHEN A ROCK WILL DO

Hard to read? You bet. Even worse, you need Flash to run this page. Try to imagine a piece of junk mail that won't let you open it because you're wearing the wrong kind of glasses!

This company has a virtual monopoly on a tiny market (home theater vibration units as well as underwater speakers) but is still willing to alienate potential customers by dissing their computer setup.

That's a banana. Pretty clear what the deal is here. No artists were injured in the creation of this ad.

EVERY ONCE IN A WHILE,
IT'S OKAY TO USE A POP-UP

As you probably know, Satan himself invented pop-up screens. These diabolical interrupters are a fast track to visitor defection.

But here, for once, is a great pop-up.

I got to the shopping cart on partsexpress.com (a great etailer, by the way, with a puzzling name) and got this message.

I'll admit, I stopped and thought, "What else could I buy to add five dollars to my cart?"

I didn't really want a clock radio, but I felt bad about missing the prize by just a few bucks.

Previous Next Reply Reply All Forward Delete Attachments

From: customerservice@mygeek.com
Date: Tue, Nov 7, 2000, 11:22 AM
To: sethgodin@yahoo.com
Subject: Thanks for using myGeek.com!, MSG-195185

Thanks for shopping with myGeek.com! We received your request for Other Home Audio Components and want you to know... we're on it!

myGeek works like this:

1. You post a request.
(You already did that, and it was pretty darn simple, eh?)

2. Your request is sent to our network of Sellers for a week.
(We already did that, and you didn't even notice!)

3. Our Sellers send replies back to try to win your business.
(They're working on it right now, even!)

4. We'll forward their replies to you via e-mail.
(You might have a Seller reply already!)

What's this mean to you?
It means that myGeek.com is about giving you more choices to buy what you're looking for. It means that you'll have more time for fun things instead of spending hours scouring the net yourself. It means that while we scurry behind the cyber scenes, you can rest assured (or go play) knowing that we're on the job for you!

Just so you know, your request, and only your request, has been sent to our Sellers. Shopping with myGeek.com is totally confidential. Absolutely none, nada, zero of your personal information is divulged to our Sellers, the IRS, the FBI, the KGB, your mother-in-law or anyone else!

...So keep a keen eye on your e-mail! Away from home? Seller quotes will also be on your personal "my Account <http://www.mygeek.com/request_overview.jsp?cust_mailid=sethgodin@yahoo.com> " page. How cool!

myGeek.com <http://www.mygeek.com/>
Your Personal Shopper

     P.S. We always made straight A's in school... how about now? E-mail us at customerservice@mygeek.com <mailto:customerservice@mygeek.com> and let us know what you think of your myGeek.com experience. **Reference**: 195185

Price: BEST PRICE
Quantity: 1
Description:

Fast and simple and obvious.

YOUR EMAIL SHOULD BE ME-MAIL

People don't want to get mail from you about you. They want to get mail from you about them.

Here's an unformatted, no graphics, no HTML, simple and fast email I got from myGeek.com. I received it about one minute after I posted a request to their site.

They created the dialogue on the web so that this mail would be exactly what I expected it would be. They didn't overpromise. They didn't generalize.

Nice.

| Previous | Next | Reply | Reply All | Forward | Delete | Attachments |

From: milan@equityengine.com
Date: Thu, Nov 2, 2000, 11:07 AM
Subject: Attend a Red Herring event for free!

Beth,

I don't know whether you saw this, but Red Herring is offering a chance to win a free trip to their "Capital Matters" conference in New York City, December 4-5. To enter, all you need to do is subscribe to one of their FREE E-newsletters like Personal Capital or Catch of the Day.

Visit http://www.eprize.net/redherring_sweeps.htm to enter the contest. Hurry, the contest ends soon!

Cleverly done, but if it were really a personal note to me, I probably would know who it was from, and they wouldn't have used a blind cc line, right?

BRAND RAGE. IT'S NOT PRETTY.

When well-known brands (*Red Herring* is a popular magazine about the new economy) stoop to sending artfully crafted spam that is not really supposed to look like spam, we've got trouble.

Spam, as I'm sure you've heard from me and others, is selfish. It's unanticipated, impersonal, irrelevant junk that steals from the recipient. Your time is valuable, and spam takes it away.

A lot of folks ignore spam. They view it as pretty benign and don't get bent out of shape.

Others, including yours truly, throw a fit. And that undoes all the hard work you've done in building your brand, doesn't it?

What are the chances that I will ever attend a *Red Herring* conference now? That I'll go out of my way to run an ad or subscribe to the magazine?

There's a reason that the great marketers of our time have avoided spam. It's not like the plague. It is the plague.

Note that "Start Search" is on the left-hand side, while the instruction that tells you to press "Start Search" is on the top, in the middle. The buttons are in the wrong places and are the wrong size and color as well.

MY BIG SECRET

I probably shouldn't tell you this, because it's such a great idea, but I will.

If you ever have to design a page like this—with plenty of buttons and lots of options that people are only going to see a few times—this tip will pay for itself the very first time you use it.

First, take a look at this page. Note that there are pull-downs, buttons with type, category choices across the top, boxes to fill in and on and on. Lots of hierarchy. Very confusing.

Now, try to imagine this. You print the page on Epson flexible magnetic paper. It's thick paper with a magnet embedded in it, sort of like Magnetic Poetry.

Cut every element on the page into a separate piece. Throw out every element that you don't absolutely need.

Take the rest of the pieces and put them on the fridge (watch out for the engineers fighting over who gets the last Jolt cola). Then rearrange all the pieces to your heart's content until you have something you like.

Even better, do it on a white board (the metal ones will hold a magnet). Then you can scribble in the pieces that are missing.

Don't you feel better already?

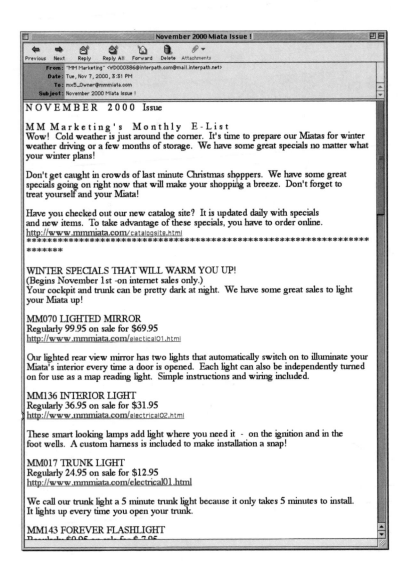

Previous   Next   Reply   Reply All   Forward   Delete   Attachments

From: "MM Marketing" <WD000386@interpath.com@mail.interpath.net>
Date: Tue, Nov 7, 2000, 3:31 PM
To: mx5_Owner@mmmiata.com
Subject: November 2000 Miata Issue !

NOVEMBER 2000 Issue

MM Marketing's Monthly E-List

Wow! Cold weather is just around the corner. It's time to prepare our Miatas for winter weather driving or a few months of storage. We have some great specials no matter what your winter plans!

Don't get caught in crowds of last minute Christmas shoppers. We have some great specials going on right now that will make your shopping a breeze. Don't forget to treat yourself and your Miata!

Have you checked out our new catalog site? It is updated daily with specials and new items. To take advantage of these specials, you have to order online.
http://www.mmmiata.com/catalogsite.html
****
****

WINTER SPECIALS THAT WILL WARM YOU UP!
(Begins November 1st -on internet sales only.)
Your cockpit and trunk can be pretty dark at night. We have some great sales to light your Miata up!

MM070 LIGHTED MIRROR
Regularly 99.95 on sale for $69.95
http://www.mmmiata.com/electrical01.html

Our lighted rear view mirror has two lights that automatically switch on to illuminate your Miata's interior every time a door is opened. Each light can also be independently turned on for use as a map reading light. Simple instructions and wiring included.

MM136 INTERIOR LIGHT
Regularly 36.95 on sale for $31.95
http://www.mmmiata.com/electrical02.html

These smart looking lamps add light where you need it - on the ignition and in the foot wells. A custom harness is included to make installation a snap!

MM017 TRUNK LIGHT
Regularly 24.95 on sale for $12.95
http://www.mmmiata.com/electrical01.html

We call our trunk light a 5 minute trunk light because it only takes 5 minutes to install. It lights up every time you open your trunk.

MM143 FOREVER FLASHLIGHT

THIS IS NOT SPAM

I asked for it.

It was anticipated, personal and relevant. I read it. I even ordered from it.

The text loads fast. It was timely. It included a link to an article I really needed.

This isn't a book about email, but when someone gets it right, he deserves credit.

If you had a newsletter like this, do you think you could turn your existing traffic into something more valuable? And if you could increase the allowable you spend on each person who visits, then you could buy more visitors!

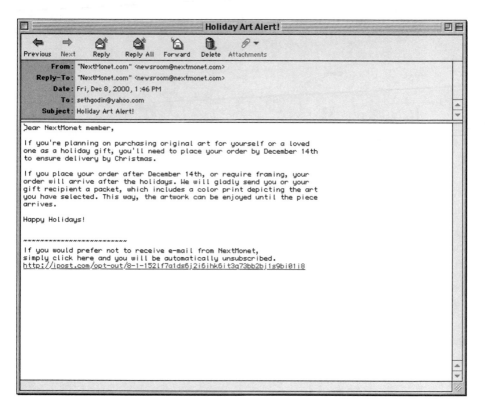

Holiday Art Alert!

Previous Next Reply Reply All Forward Delete Attachments

From: "NextMonet.com" <newsroom@nextmonet.com>
Reply-To: "NextMonet.com" <newsroom@nextmonet.com>
Date: Fri, Dec 8, 2000, 1:46 PM
To: sethgodin@yahoo.com
Subject: Holiday Art Alert!

Dear NextMonet member,

If you're planning on purchasing original art for yourself or a loved one as a holiday gift, you'll need to place your order by December 14th to ensure delivery by Christmas.

If you place your order after December 14th, or require framing, your order will arrive after the holidays. We will gladly send you or your gift recipient a packet, which includes a color print depicting the art you have selected. This way, the artwork can be enjoyed until the piece arrives.

Happy Holidays!

~~~~~~~~~~~~~~~~~~~~~~~
If you would prefer not to receive e-mail from NextMonet, simply click here and you will be automatically unsubscribed.
http://ipost.com/opt-out/8-1-152lf7a1ds6j2i6ihk6it3q73bb2bj1s9bi01i8

Where's the link? Let's say this email actually got opened (I'm not crazy about the hyperbolic subject line, but that's a different story). Where would I click?

TRUE CONFESSION

Everybody makes mistakes.

Everybody posts a web site with the wrong data on it, or sends an email to thousands of loyal fans but forgets to include the link that was the entire purpose of the mail.

It's okay. I do it too.

Send yourself email before you send it to a large group of folks.

Send it to your boss while you're at it.

```
----------
From: <oprah-editor@amazon.com>
Date: Tue, 27 Feb 2001 17:34:50 -0800 (PST)
To: "oprah-subscribers"
Subject: An Apology to Our Oprah Book Club Subscribers


Dear Amazon Subscriber,

How does that old song go? You know, "You say po-tay-to, I say
po-tah-to, you say to-may-to, I say to-mah-to."

It looks like you said "Oprah," and we heard, well, "opera." Last
night we accidentally sent our "Amazon.com Delivers Opera & Vocal
Grammy Winners" e-mail to you, our Oprah Book Club(R) subscribers.

Please note that you are still subscribed to our Oprah Book Club
Delivers list. You have not been subscribed to our Opera & Vocal
Delivers list, and will receive no more opera e-mail. (Unless, of
course, Oprah takes up opera.)

We apologize for any inconvenience this may have caused.

Sincerely,

Keith Walsh
Amazon.com Delivers Manager
```

No, I'm not an Amazon apologist. This proves it.

WHEN YOU DO SCREW UP . . .

Please have a sense of humor about it.

Unless you're doing online dialysis, it's unlikely that you're dealing with matters of life and death. If Hotmail lost someone's entire email folder, that would be a different story entirely.

So, when you make a mistake, own up to it. Apologize. And do it with a smile.

This is the funniest email I've seen in a while. Anyone can make a mistake, and I think you'll be pleasantly surprised at how forgiving customers are if you break your string of otherwise exceptional customer service with a goof now and then.

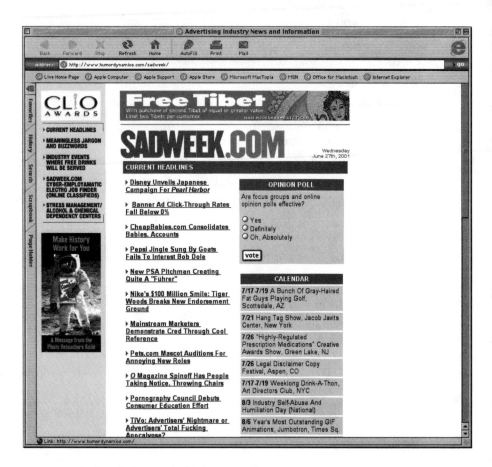

It doesn't have to be boring to work.

IT'S NOT ALWAYS ABOUT YOU

Most web sites are exercises in narcissism. Me, me, me, the site proclaims. But I don't care about you or your company. I care about me!

Here's a site from modernhumorist.com. Instead of announcing their new miniagency (Humor Dynamics) with a press release or a boring site, they put their money where their mouth is and built a parody.

This site parodies a leading advertising trade magazine, meaning that it's of most interest to their target market—people who read advertising trade magazines!

With riffs like "Free Tibet (with purchase of second Tibet of equal or greater value)," the site is guaranteed to make even a hard-boiled ad guy smile. And probably send it on to a friend as well.

I found this site through word of mouse, and most visitors will too. Click on any of the sidebar links, though, and the fun and games stop (well, just a little—these guys are nuts) and the selling starts. That's okay, though, because this site already sold me on why they're great and it's relevant to their message.

Want to know what makes fatwallet.com a profit? It's the top links in the most popular box, as well as the deals of the day. By highlighting the best ones, they dramatically increase their return on investment.

IF YOU MEASURE IT, IT GETS DONE

After reading the first edition of *The Big Red Fez,* the person behind fatwallet.com did a very simple thing. He rearranged the site to put his most profitable links near the top. And he started measuring.

Within a week, profit from his best links increased more than 200 percent.

It's so simple. Measure what you want to happen and then test to make the measurements go up. If it's that easy, why doesn't everyone do it?

Good question.

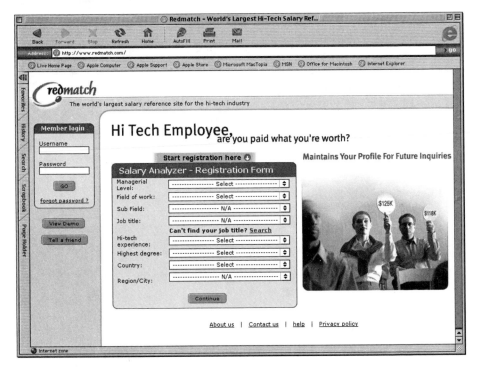

If you have any doubts about exactly what this site is for and how to use it, perhaps this is the wrong industry for you.

EDIT, EDIT, EDIT

It's hard to see how this site could be more straightforward—
yet it's professional and inviting at the same time.

There's no doubt in my mind that the folks at Red-
match.com had to go through hundreds of iterations to get
this right. But once you do get it right, it's so obvious you
wonder why it took you so long.

Here's a tip: No need to invent the wheel. Someone has
come before you and done most of the work. Find the sites on
the web that are working and copy their organization. It's
good for you and the users as well.

The big finale. Not only is there a banana here, and a fun, easy-to-use interface, but this site is very profitable and very, very cheap. Nice work.

BEING CHEAP AND STILL GETTING IT RIGHT

This site blew me away. Even if you don't like teddy bears, it makes you want to order one for someone who does.

But it's not just the appealing design and obvious measurement that makes this site the last in the book. It's how cheap it was.

According to their webmaster, they do $20 million a year in sales, with some days exceeding $1 million. Even better, they do it with a site that costs four thousand dollars (not a misprint) a year to serve, running software they bought for five thousand dollars.

What do they do with the hundreds of thousands of dollars they didn't spend with Scient or Viant or Exodus? They buy radio ads. Then they track the ads and only run the ones that work.

The Yahoo! store and some common sense may be all you need to run a profitable business on the Internet. Have fun.

RECOMMENDED SITES

www.thebigredfez.com	Contribute new URLs
www.ideavirus.com	Sign up for a free newsletter
www.thebigredfez.com/books	Find books by Seth Godin
www.permission.com/sethbio	Find Seth's biography
www.greatertalent.com	Find Seth's speaker's bureau
www.designfactorynet.com	Find Red Maxwell

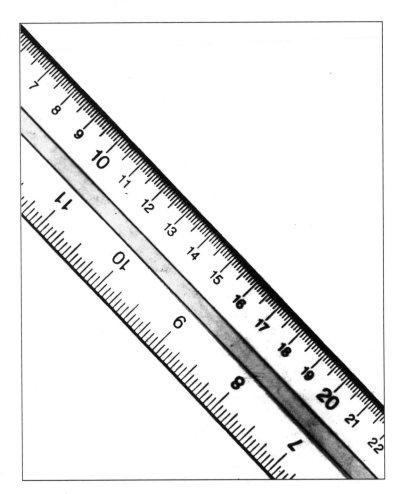

Test and measure.

ACKNOWLEDGMENTS AND CONTACTS

Thanks to Sam and Erick and Jeff at Amazon. And to the folks at Flatiron, Lark Productions, Yahoo!, Yoyodyne, Kern, Greater Talent, Hyperion and Hard Manufacturing. Thanks also to Lisa Considine at Fireside and Fred Hills at The Free Press for having the vision to bring this book, kicking and screaming, to paper.

Special thanks to Robin, Lisa and Karen.

If you'd like to contact Greater Talent Network about a speaking engagement, please visit www.greatertalent.com.

For a list of consultants, artists and designers that "get" the Big Red Fez, go to www.designfactorynet.com.

To submit your own banana riff, visit www.bigredfez.com.

All of my proceeds from the sale of this book are being donated to the Juvenile Diabetes Foundation. If you'd like to contribute as well, their site is at www.jdf.org.

Thanks for reading.

One more thing: I'm only sure of one thing about your web site:

It's not as good as it could be, but if you test it, it will get better.

THE BIG RED FEZ

ABOUT THE AUTHOR

Promo Magazine called Seth "The Prime Minister of Permission Marketing," and *Fortune* chose *Permission Marketing* as one of their Best Business Books. The book was an Amazon.com top one hundred bestseller for a year, and it spent four months on the *Business Week* bestseller list.

Godin's last book was *Unleashing the Ideavirus*. More than a million people have downloaded the digital version, making it the most popular ebook ever. Featured in *USA Today, The New York Times, The Industry Standard* and *Wired Online,* this book broke new ground in the way ideas are distributed. It is now available in bookstores nationwide.

He is also a columnist for *Fast Company,* writing about change and how corporations and individuals can successfully deal with the massive rifts our economy is facing.

Godin is a renowned speaker as well. He is ranked as the number-one speaker of the more than two thousand people who have presented at Internet World over the last five years, and was chosen as one of twenty-one Speakers for the Next Century by *Successful Meetings.*

Seth was founder and CEO of Yoyodyne, the industry's leading interactive direct-marketing company, which Yahoo! acquired in late 1998.

He holds an MBA from Stanford and was called "the Ultimate Entrepreneur for the Information Age" by *Business Week.*

Find a current bio by clicking on www.permission.com/sethbio.